2. ENGINE FAILURE — Error! Bookmark not defined.
3. PATIENCE — Error! Bookmark not defined.
4. SELF-REPAIRS — Error! Bookmark not defined.
5. LOVE YA! — Error! Bookmark not defined.
6. PRETTY PASSENGERS — Error! Bookmark not defined.
7. CAPTAIN KIRK — Error! Bookmark not defined.
8. ARRIVAL — Error! Bookmark not defined.
9. EPILOGUE — Error! Bookmark not defined.

TT:

Train of Thought

by

V.A. / Nick Peterson

TT: Train of Thought / Adventures Beyond the Hemisphere

Copyright © 2012 V.A. Virtual Alien/Nick Peterson under licence to The Edge Press/DiaryUnlimited. All rights reserved. AnotherClip.com

ISBN-13: 978-0-9526607-4-3

DiaryUnlimited.com

CONTENTS

Contents

1. DEPARTURE 8

2. ENGINE FAILURE 16

3. PATIENCE 23

4. SELF-REPAIRS 30

5. LOVE YA! 32

6. PRETTY PASSENGERS 38

7. CAPTAIN KIRK 41

8. ARRIVAL 46

9. EPILOGUE 48

Characters

Group 1 - 2 English middle accent G1 (group) M1 (male) G1 (group) F1
(female)
Group 2 - 3 American English - NY accent. G2- M1, M2, F1
Group 3 - 1 Australian, 1 Scot, 1 English-middle accent, 1 Welsh M1-4
Group 4 - 2 American - MidWest accent G4F1, G4F2

The train driver (only heard through the speakers)
A clear "campy" and articulate voice and if used in excess can seriously injure anyone in the vicinity, especially if trapped inside a train with no chance of an escape.

The "Refreshment" boy staff
The "Refreshment" girl staff
Two men, the last passengers to leave the train at the end

1 narrator

Situation and Set
The whole story is set inside a train carriage. Due to an engine failure the journey is dragging on without knowing when it will end. The only information received is from the "camp" voice of the main train driver blasting away throughout the train at regular intervals. The passengers are forced to endure this, pushing them to the limits; into some deep agonising fits and often deeply traumatic moments.

Lips Reading

When the passengers are forced to endure the train driver's announcements, their bewilderments are clearly visible throughout their faces (When the train driver's voice is heard) and during these scenes their voices have been muted and instead along with the view on each passenger's face, a zooming on each pair of lips offer a fairly accurate comprehension of their speech and reactions. (Subtitles added when dubbed in foreign languages will provide the same effect).

Each lip is from each group of passengers. One single lip recovers the whole screen but sometimes all the lips are merged together on the same screen and the lips reading exercise continues in synchronised effect.

SUMMARY

Inside a train carriage of an average size, average train, somewhere in the world, somewhere in time; it's a gruelling journey of two hours, perhaps four hours with many unexpected stops and slow-downs due to engine failure, as many trains tend to these days.

The train leaves its destination slightly late. It is not a full train; there is only a group of four parties who boarded the carriage. There is plenty of space to allow some room to move and plenty of empty seats between each group of people.

They all converse with one another. There is: - a group of 2, - a group of 3, - a group of 4 and another group of two in that order.

During the journey they all speak to each other either together and in unison or they are responding to their own respective conversation without even acknowledging their receiver's end conversation all veering deep to what is in fact their own monologue. No one is really listening to what the other one has to say but the interaction is still vibrant, and often high-ended. Towards the end, it's almost as if all the passengers were talking to a brick wall; but the difference is that a brick hasn't got a face or a sound. All the groups share the same conversation but never interact between and with the different groups. They only share the same train of thought(s).

Before the train arrives at its final destination each group merges to include their own respective conversation and finally reply to each other and argue within the actual topic of the conversation.

There is a train of thought floating around between each group during the journey and it seems between all the groups inside the carriage. The train journey is interrupted several times when the train has stopped and the voice of the train driver is heard through the speakers. During the long and often agonising and irritating sets of announcements the passengers have all been muted but the general mood is reflected over their faces.

1. DEPARTURE: INTRODUCING THE TRAIN DRIVER

<u>Scene 1</u>

When the sound of a bell is played an announcement by the train driver is heard. All the parties then stop talking. There is a deep silence emerging from the carriage but their emotions and expressions are reflected on their faces as they hear the news bulletins from the train driver.

The train driver

Let me introduce myself: I'm blond, blue eyes, some say handsome and I'm your train driver this evening. Lucky people you are!

Lips Reading G1
F1

What?

The train driver

We have two services for refreshments on the train rolling around as I speak. One pretty girl and one pretty boy. More luck for you there! As my uncle Anatole used to say.

Lips Reading G1
M1

Confused
???????

The train driver

Have a tremendous journey!

Scene 2

G1

F1

She did it all night...

M1

It must have been lightning

F1

Honestly, *shaking her head and glancing at him* the way she went about it...

M1

A touch of Dutch Elm disease as well!

F1

But he's so vain...

M1

Such a shame...

F1

For fuck's sake, you know raising *her voice he* did it!

M1

Raising his voice, staring at her
All the trees burnt to their roots!

F1

Shaking her head in disbelief and half looking at the window
I don't believe you sometimes!

M1

It's genocide!

F1

What the hell were you thinking? That's what I'd like to know!

M1

Dutch Elm disease or some French stuff, foreign anyway!

F1

Let me text him and we'll see what she's saying a *few seconds later*

M1

I've received a garbled message from Kat. She's not angry about what I have said to you. Whatever that means...

F1

My mother told me to ignore her...

M1

How can she possibly know what I did?

F1

That's what I'd like to know!

M1

He wouldn't want me to go there...

F1

Yes, she would...

M1

Fuck him! I've got better things to do with my time!

F1

She means well...

M1

I'm sure he means well

F1

She's into Madonna, this old bag!

M1

He's into bloody Lady Gaga!

F1

There's no hope for her

M1

There's no hope for him

F1

At least he's not into Gaga!

M1

At least she's not into that Madonna thing. My granny used to be into Madonna.

F1

She's not too young but not too old either.

V.A.

Scene 3

In the middle of the carriage

G2

M1

As the fucking Brits down the carriage would say: "You can't even run a piss in a brewery!"

F1

I thought about it for a long time and I did think I could do it!

M2

A step backwards in your arrogance wouldn't go amiss

F1

Shouting
That's fucking rich coming from a self-centred *shaking her head* pretentious brain dead *losing her rather long oblong hard to ignore earrings; all falling on the floor and she bows down to fetch them*

M1

That's what I have to put up with *stuffing a few crisps in his mouth* while the people *continue with a mouth full* at work *grabbing each side of the bag by the top very tightly and breaking the (big) pack of crisps and lifting the packet of crisps. In a split second all the crisps have been scattered up in the air. All the crisps ended up on the floor, on the seats and over his receivers' end faces.*

F1

I rest my case removing *debris of crisps stuck over her face*

M2

He removes the crisps from his coat and then he sits down.
If I was him, I would have worn a giant condom.

M1

With a mouth full of crisps
Nothing can protect other trees from foreign invasions.

F1

I dread to think what disease she caught...

M2

In real terms, trees are being castrated...

M1

Chop the balls of the old dog!

M2

They'll never grow again!

F2

He won't infect anyone anymore!

2. ENGINE FAILURE

Scene 4

The train driver
Due to an engine failure the train will slow down for a short while then hopefully we will resume our journey. You're safe in my hands. My professional responsibilities are to carry out all procedures and policies as set by the management, to maintain high standards ensuring the health, safety and welfare of the clients. That's you…

Lips Reading
G2M1
What the fuck…

There is complete silence in the train whilst the train driver communicates his latest announcement. A sense of complete bewilderment is clearly visible on everyone's face.

The train driver
…And I have to be able to manage people effectively to achieve the best results and have management skills at a high level – in this field acumen is imperative-. An understanding of change in management as well as crisis management is essential, together with a good awareness of management control. As I will be in constant contact with all the

passengers, interpersonal and people skills will go hand in hand with my personal skills. And that's how I got into the job in the first place!

Lips Reading

Recovering the whole screen

G3M1

Fuck me!

The train driver

As my Uncle Anatole used to say: better the devil you know and by now I'm sure you've been quite acquainted with me!

Lips Reading
G3M2

Recovering the whole screen
What the fuck?

Scene 5

G3

M1

The cost of living is so dear...

M2

He was away

M3

Right...

M4

Stupid oaf!

M1

In the end...

M2

No way!

TT: Train of Thought

M3

I get it up in no time!

M4

Calibration...

M1

I'm all for it...

M2

And bang inside

M3

Slowly does it

M4

God I'm desperate

M1

Through a hole

M2

Solid and strong

M3

Do it to me

M4

Yes

V.A.

M1

Stop this

M2

When you're desperate!

M3

So much for self-support

M4

Accordingly, ...

M1

I went through it

M2

Let's face it, when...

M3

You're not listening

M4

I want it out!

M1

I'm saying all through it

M2

All over your face!

M3

Getting angry, raising his voice
Listen!

M4

Out from behind!

M1

Deep end

M2

Then counter attack

M3

Angrier
That's your fucking problem!

M4

But slowly...

M1

Determined
And pushing this...

M2

...and feeling laid back!

M3

Moron!

V.A.

M4

Happy ever after!

The train slows down again to a complete halt. The group is suddenly confronted to face the final phase of their conversation. The only part of the whole screenplay where there is some link in the conversation.

M1 (English)

Abdean?

M2 (Australian)

Where?

M3 (Welsh)

Aberdeen!

M4 (Scot)

Aber-bloody-deen!

M1 (English)

Oh yeah… It's a town in Scotland!

---

3. PATIENCE

Scene 6

The train driver

The engine is still a problem. It's a shame because we were just about to restart.

Lips Reading
G2F1

No, really?

The train driver

I wonder what triggered the re-start. We will try to minimise the delay. I keep on pushing the engine but it's a problem. It will restart in time. We just have to wait and be patient.

Lips Reading
G2M1

Gimme a fucking gun and I'll fucking kill ya!

V.A.

The train driver

As my uncle Anatole used to say: patience is the mother of all virtue.

Lips Reading G1M1

I'll fucking have you with your Uncle Ana what's his face!

The train driver

Well, I'll keep you posted! Bye for now!

Meanwhile the passengers continue their conversations.

Scene 7

G2

F1

Was he married?

M1

He lived with a donkey

M2

I'm not surprised!

F1

What are they talking about?

M1

Is she deaf?

M2

She loves Justin Bieber!

V.A.

F1

That explains it

M1 *Worried and concerned*

I can't begin to imagine...

M2

Visibly shaken

Why am I doing this?

F1

So horrendous

M1

He is

M2

Don't you know?

F1

Above average

M1

She's a prostitute!

M2

Yes, He is all right

F1

Beneath the surface

M1

Really, she sucks!

M1

He does it!

M2

All the way?

F1

Deep down at throat level.

M1

He got a cold.

M2

You're having me on!

F1

No, no

M1

It's true!

M2

So, elaborate

V.A.

F1

He doesn't even need any special advice

M1

He just does it

M2

She does. She really does!

F1

Knowing what I know…

M1

Thinking what I'm thinking…

M2

Moving the way, he moves…

F1

Wagging his tail, the way he does…

M1

And all these … *coughing*

M2

Feeling this urge… *coughing*

F1

Not knowing… *coughing*

M1

Needing... *coughing*

They all cough hysterically for half a minute with G2 gradually switching the cough to a frantic and uncontrollable laugh, swiftly followed by the other groups for a whole minute.

4. SELF-REPAIRS

Scene 8

The train driver
Hi there! This is your captain speaking. It's me! We've moved on a bit.

Lips Reading
G1M1

For fuck's sake!

The train driver
We will get to our destination at some point in time.

Lips Reading

Screaming
Then get in on!

The train driver
No, only me. Just kidding. It's still the engine. I'm still working on it. It took me a while to find a spanner.

Lips Reading

What the fuck?

The train driver

There was a screw loose in there but I've used a drop of glue that I got to fix it. It'll be alright.

Very fast overview of each passenger's face

The train driver

In the meantime, Ladies and gents, boys and girls, there is a pretty boy serving refreshments moving along inside the train. I'm not sure what's going on with him. I haven't heard from him in a while. OK that's all folks for now. I'll keep you posted!

All the members of G4's group are staring at each other in complete disbelief.

5. LOVE YA!

Scene 9

The train driver

I'm your man!

Lips Reading
G1M1

Piss off!

The train driver

Your driver is speaking! I haven't heard from the boy serving the refreshments. I'm really worried about him. There is also a pretty girl somewhere serving refreshments. They don't work together. They are supposed to contact me every 30 minutes for safety purposes but they have failed to do so. Something could have happened to them on duty. Anyway, I'm sure you have enough to worry about.

Lips Reading
G2M2

Screaming, mouth wide opened
Argggggh!

The train driver
By the way my Uncle Anatole…

Lips Reading
No! Not Anatole!

The train driver
The problem with my uncle Anatole is that he's not the man I thought he was...

Inside the train…
G2 M2
Raising his hands in the air in desperation!

The train driver
He never showed me any kind of affection...

G4 M2
Raising his eyebrows

The train driver
... He should have shown me as an uncle.

Lips Reading G2
F1
No, no, no!

G2 M1
Gasp!

V.A.

The train driver

I haven't been hugged as much as I believe I should have.

3 lips are appearing in split screen on the screen

G2M1

Ga, ga, ga....

G2M2

Jerk!

G2F1

Arghhh!

The train driver

I still love my Uncle Anatole but I've expected more from him.

Inside the train...

G4M1

Right hand recovering his face

G4M2

Both hands pressed over his head

G2 F1

Eyes wide shut

G2 M1
Displaying his middle finger backwards and shaking this same finger vigorously

G1M1
The train stops abruptly and he falls off from his seat.
The train driver
Oh, No! I've switched the engine off!

G3M1
Stands up and in a hysterical rage tries to open the door to the next carriage and, unable to do so, starts banging at the door followed by the rest of G1 group to the consternation of Group A seating and standing still by the door watching the proceedings.

Lips reading
All lips from G3 are displayed on the screen, recovering the screen howling abuses at the train driver.

G3
Fuck off, shithead, wanker, (repeated 3 times)

Fucking cunt, I'll fucking do you head in, shut the fuck up.
Repeated 3 times

Moron, idiot from **xxxxxxxxx (and xxxxxxx)**
(Censored)
Repeated 3 times

V.A.
Shut the fuck up you fuck face fuck, fucking crap head!
Repeated 3 times

The train driver
My uncle Anatole said that I've always been a good boy!

In perfect synchronisation, after having displayed their bewilderment over their faces, each passenger is letting their head to fall over toward their lap simultaneously from group 1 to 4.

The train is still stuck in the middle of nowhere...

The train driver
I wonder if I put oil or water over the engine this will make a difference...

Focus on G1 M1 face, eyes rolling from left to right

The train driver
I've got some Vodka here; this might do the trick...

G2F1
Focus on her face: completely transfigured with fear

The train driver
Oh No! It reads in the instruction manual: "strictly no alcohol contact with the engine"

At this precise moment in time, each passenger one by one and simultaneously, in perfect coordination is falling from its seat and they all end up on the floor.

Overview on the carnage with all the passengers on the floor, completely worn-out and in disbelief.

After one minute all of a sudden, the engine re-starts forcing some passengers to bang their heads on the walls or the floor. Some passengers have knocked themselves so badly in the process that they started to bleed...

Lips Reading

A transcript of their agony is clearly visible on everyone's lips. Each lip from each passenger is displayed on the screen from the centre and one by one all the passengers' lips recover the screen.

Their respective dialogue ranges from agony and desperation for the passengers badly bruised to hurling abuses for the remaining passengers still strong enough to do so.

Back inside the train...

The train driver

So, I'll leave you and love ya!

6. PRETTY PASSENGERS

Scene 10

Back on the train...

The train driver
How are my pretties?

Lips Reading G4M1
Cunt!

The train driver
We have moved for a long while but we have stopped again as I'm sure you've noticed.

Lips Reading G2M1
Cunt!

The train driver
It's a shame it's in the evening: there's nothing to see outside but I'm sure you can find a way to pass the hours. That reminds me of my Uncle Anatole. Have I ever told you about my Uncle Anatole?

Lips Reading
G3M1

Yes, you fucking twat!

At this precise moment the passengers are in complete disbelief. They all stand up and try frantically and desperately to open the door to the next carriage but it's still stuck.

The train driver

He's a pretty horrible fella. Tall, stupid, spotty, big nose, big lips, big mouth and...

The train suddenly reverses backwards and all the passengers standing up fall on the floor, banging parts of their bodies in the process and they are all in agony whilst trying to get up.

The train driver

Ooops! Sorry about that! I've reversed!

Lips Reading G2M1
Fucking Jerk!

Lips Reading G2M2
I'm gonna fucking kill ya!

The train driver
Now the engine is working again. That's a relief. We're off! By now!

7. CAPTAIN KIRK

Scene 11

The train driver
Captain Kirk speaking!

Lips Reading G2F1
Nooooooo!

Lips Reading G1F1
Please, no!

The train driver
Boys and girls! We've moved!

Lips Reading G3M2
Moron!

Lips Reading G3M2
I'll fucking have you!

The train driver

Not far off to our destination but got stuck again. Maybe we could all get off now and push the train! How about that? Haha!

The lips are appearing one by one on the screen and eventually all the following ten lips continue their short dialogue at the same time. In the first set of lips each passenger utters one swear word and in the second set they are all screaming abuses at the train driver.

Lips Reading

Lips Reading

Lips Reading

Lips Reading

Lips Reading

Lips Reading

Lips Reading

Lips Reading

Lips Reading

Lips Reading

**Lips Reading Lips Reading Lips Reading Lips Reading
Lips Reading Lips Reading Lips Reading Lips Reading
Lips Reading Lips Reading Lips Reading**

The train driver

Only kidding! You honestly didn't think that I, your beloved captain would have let you out; you; my pretties in the cold of the night?

G4 with a parade of swear words.

Lips Reading

Lips Reading

Lips Reading

Lips Reading

The train driver

Anyway, what happened to the refreshment staff? They should have given a sign of life hours ago. Has anyone seen them? I hope they are still alive on this train. That reminds me: is anyone missing or might have disappeared? If this is the case, press the alarm! But this will also slow down the train... again! You can never win, can't you?

All together now, swearing more abuses at the train driver:

                Lips Reading

                Lips Reading

                Lips Reading

                Lips Reading

                Lips Reading

                Lips Reading

                Lips Reading

                Lips Reading

                Lips Reading

                Lips Reading

The train driver suddenly bursts into a hysterical fit of laughter. For a whole minute this is met with complete disbelief from the passengers. After one minute of this the train departs again for the last time.

TT: Train of Thought
The train driver
Ah! Funny that was! You're such a nice bunch! Anyway, we're off to our final destination. It's been an experience. I love you all!

8. ARRIVAL

Scene 12

The train driver
Houston, the Eagle has landed!

Lips Reading

Lips Reading

Lips Reading

Lips Reading

Lips Reading

Lips Reading

Lips Reading

Lips Reading

Lips Reading

Lips Reading

All the previous lips representing all the passengers are now merging together and recovering the screen.

Lips Reading Lips Reading Lips Reading Lips Reading Lips Reading Lips Reading Lips Reading Lips Reading Lips Reading Lips Reading Lips Reading

9. EPILOGUE

Everyone leaves the train; slowly, completely annihilated, some heavily bruised and like a group of zombies, they all leave the train not really realising where they have arrived or what the hell happened in the train.

As soon as the last passenger has left the train, there are some strange sounds coming from the next carriage; the noise is coming from inside the male toilet/washroom cubicle and from the female toilet/washroom cubicle opposite.

1st washroom/toilet:

First male voice: [noises Rated R in the U.S. and 18 in the UK]

Additional dialogue:
This way/Oh, really that's interesting! /I would have thought…/ Evidently…/Oh not that hard, that hurts!

First female voice (the refreshment girl):
[noises Rated R in the U.S. and 18 in the UK]

Additional dialogue:
Just biting across/I'm hungry

2nd washroom/ toilet:

> **First male voice:** [noises Rated R in the U.S. and 18 in the UK]

Oh dear/You are a bit of a rebel/Desperate, are you? /That's right!

Additional dialogue:

> **Second male voice (the refreshment boy)**
[noises Rated R in the U.S. and 18 in the UK]

Give it all!

A few seconds later…

1st toilet:

The door suddenly opens slowly and the female "refreshment" staff gets out.

> **Second female voice:**
I think we have arrived. The coast is clear…

She leaves the carriage, then the train is soon followed by a man a few seconds later. Then opposite the then mentioned toilet/washroom cubicle, the "refreshment" boy staff slowly and hesitantly opens the door and his face sneaks out.

Second male voice (the refreshment boy)
I think the coast is clear. We must have arrived.

He walks back inside the cubicle for a few seconds.

Second male voice (the refreshment boy)
See ya!

He then walks out, leaves the carriage, the train and the story. He is followed a few seconds later by another man coming straight out from the washroom/cubicle.

Epilogue (and possibly the same for the prologue) narrated over the screen.

The passengers are sharing their thoughts with everyone. Every single passenger is an open book. No one knows it. They are all transparent. They can't unlock what is passing through their mind; it's the train of thought. It comes and it goes, it ricochets from one passenger to another in a different form, a different word or sentence but in the end, it's always the same conversation.

The End.

NOTES

1. For the actors playing the refreshment boy and girl and their respective partners, it will enhance the end by having "guest stars".

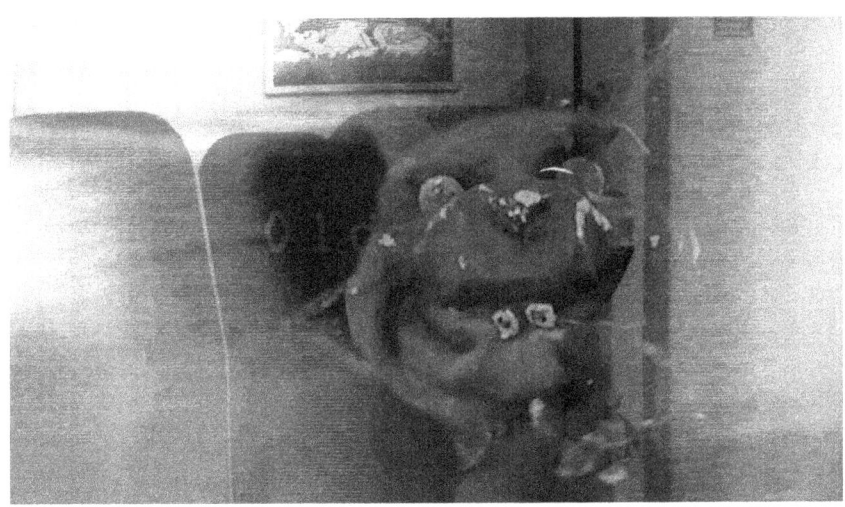

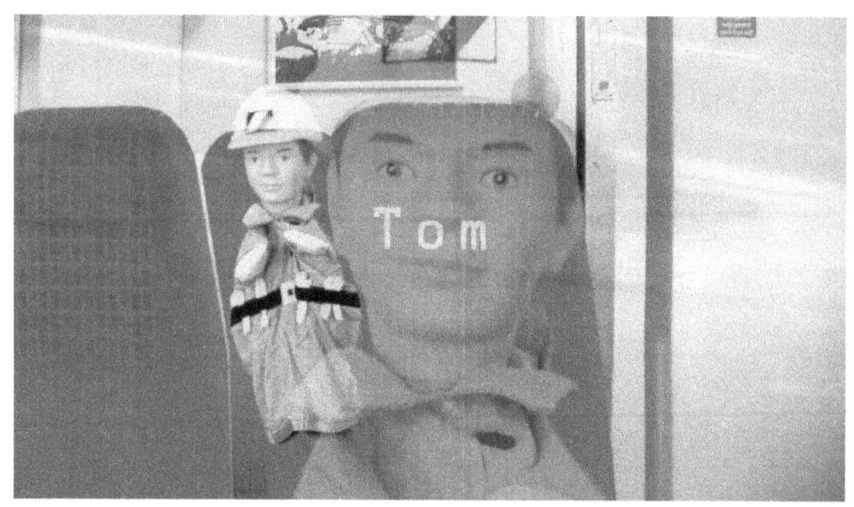

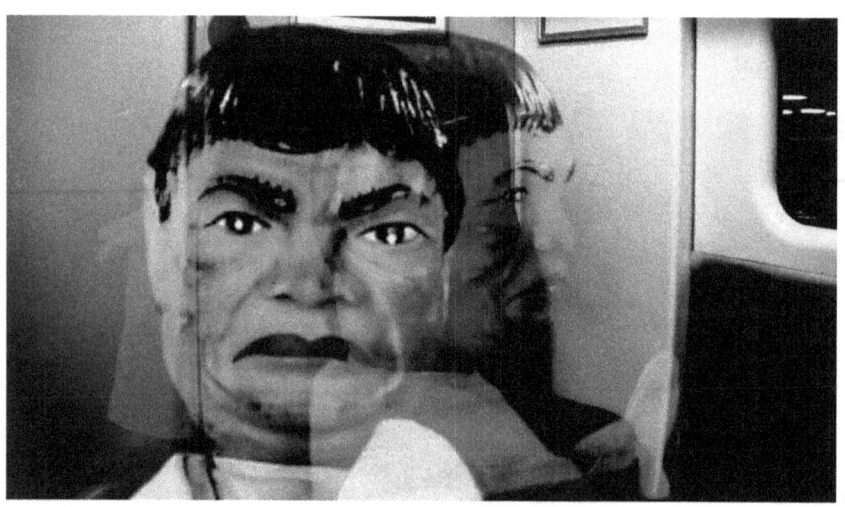

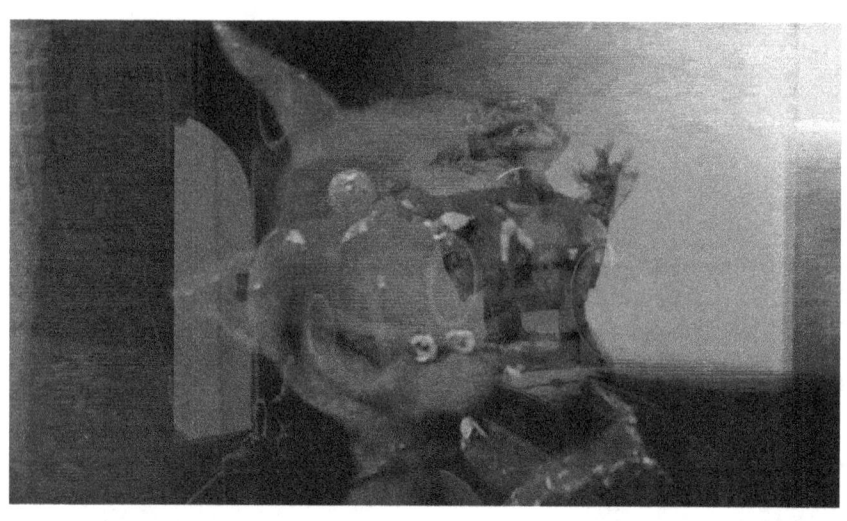

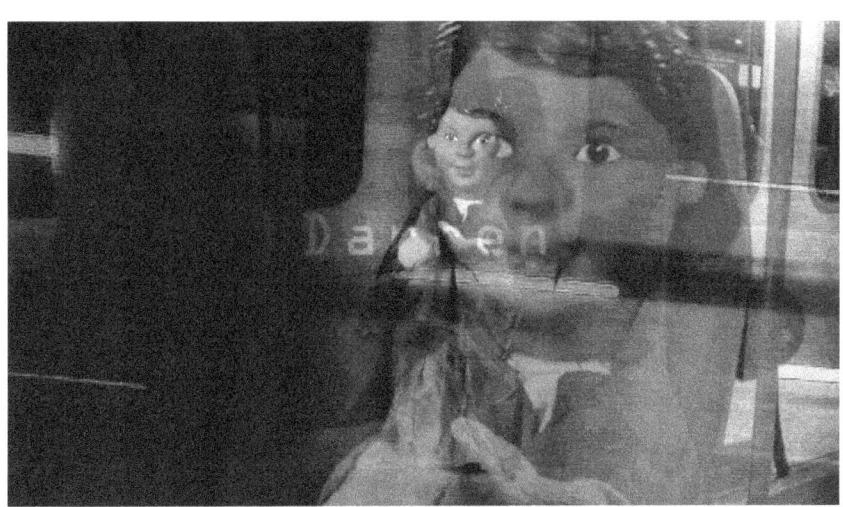

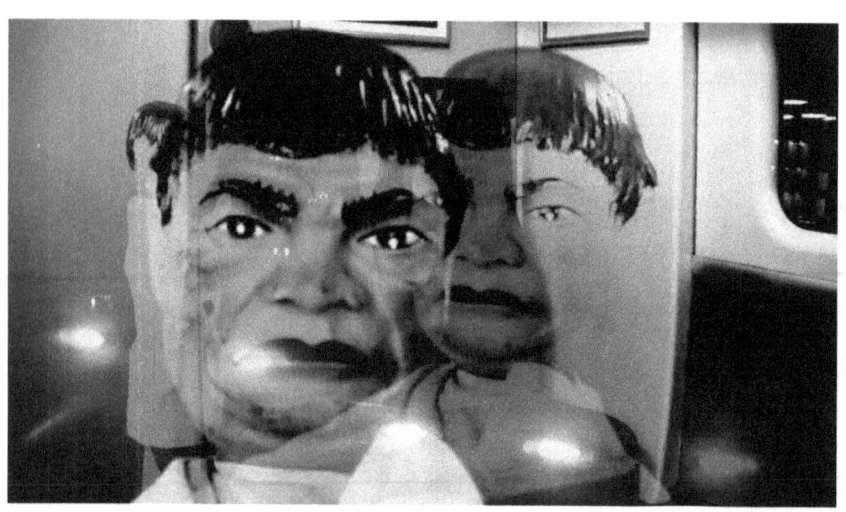

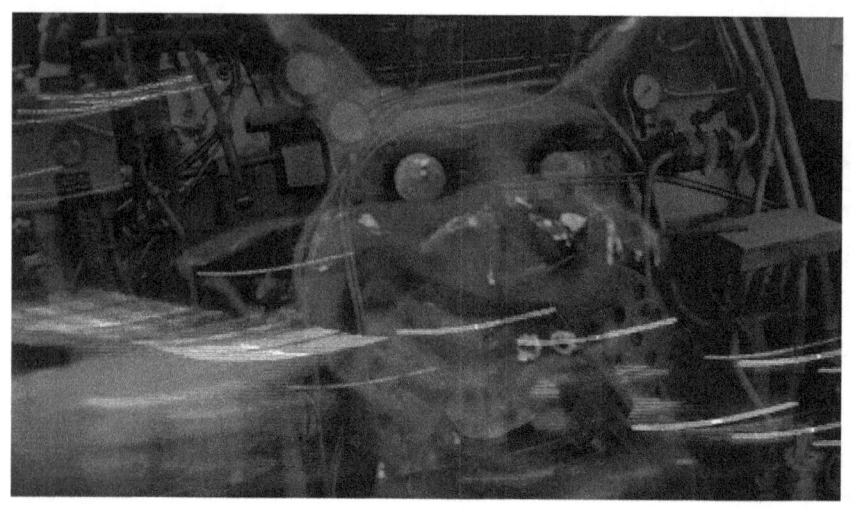

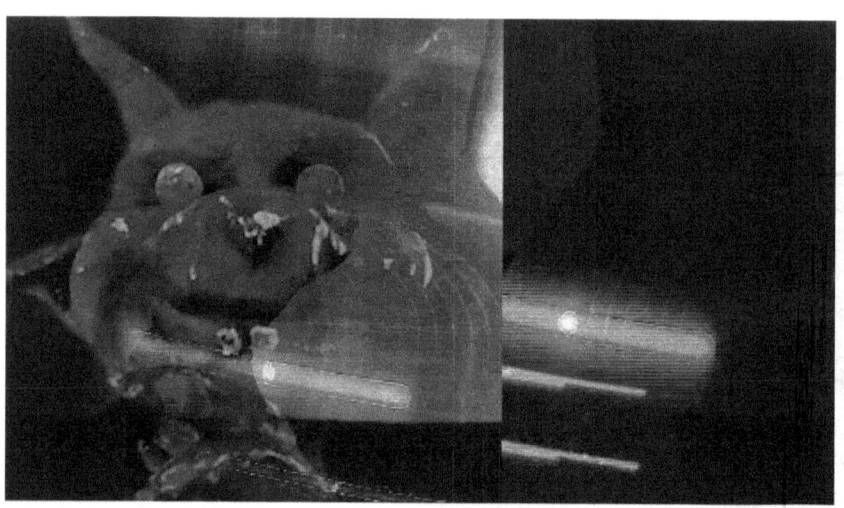

www.ingramcontent.com/pod-product-compliance
Lightning Source LLC
Chambersburg PA
CBHW032100150426
43194CB00006B/599